VALLEY 8/27/2014 C:1
50690010977400
MacRae, Sloan.
Meet Vladimir Guerrero :
baseball's Super Vlad /

7/30/14

All-Star Players™

MEET VLADIMIR GUERRERO

Baseball's Super Vlad

Sloan MacRae

PowerKiDS
press
New York

Published in 2009 by The Rosen Publishing Group, Inc.
29 East 21st Street, New York, NY 10010

First Edition

Editor: Amelie von Zumbusch
Book Design: Greg Tucker
Photo Researcher: Jessica Gerweck

Photo Credits: Cover, pp. 4, 7, 8, 13, 14, 15, 16, 18, 21, 22, 23, 24, 28, 30 © Getty Images; p. 11 © Diamond Images/Getty Images; pp. 12, 26, 27 © MLB Photos via Getty Images; p. 19 © Associated Press.

Library of Congress Cataloging-in-Publication Data

MacRae, Sloan.
    Meet Vladimir Guerrero : baseball's Super Vlad / Sloan MacRae. — 1st ed.
        p. cm. — (All-star players)
    Includes index.
    ISBN 978-1-4358-2707-3 (library binding) — ISBN 978-1-4358-3099-8 (pbk.)
ISBN 978-1-4358-3105-6 (6-pack)
    1. Guerrero, Vladimir, 1976– —Juvenile literature. 2. Baseball players—United States—Biography—Juvenile literature. 3. Baseball players—Dominican Republic—Biography—Juvenile literature. I. Title.
    GV865.G84M33 2009
    796.357092—dc22
    [B]
                                            2008022077

Manufactured in the United States of America

Contents

Vladimir Guerrero has played for the Angels since 2004. Before that, he played for the Montreal Expos.

Speak Softly and Carry a Big Bat

Vladimir Guerrero may be a superstar, but he never brags. Guerrero is one of the best power hitters in Major League Baseball. Major League Baseball is also called MLB, or simply the majors. Guerrero plays right field for the Los Angeles Angels of Anaheim.

Guerrero comes from Latin America. Latin America has a rich baseball **tradition**. There are many Latin American baseball stars. Guerrero is one of the best. He is also probably the shyest. Many sports stars love to appear in newspapers and on TV. Guerrero is quieter than most **professional** ballplayers, though. He prefers to let his bat speak for him.

All-Star Facts

Guerrero's full name is Vladimir Alvino Guerrero.

Guerrero was born in the Dominican Republic. He had eight brothers and sisters. Guerrero's family was poor, and it was hard for his parents to feed everyone. There was no running water, so the family sometimes had to drink water from puddles on the ground. Vladimir had to quit school at a young age so that he could work.

Vladimir grew up working hard, but he played baseball when he could. He was a natural **athlete**. Vladimir's older brother, Wilton, was also an excellent baseball player. **Scouts** from the majors watched the brothers play. The Guerrero brothers never imagined that one day they would play for the same major-league team.

All-Star Facts

Baseball runs in the Guerrero family. Vladimir's youngest brother, Julio, is a professional baseball player. His cousins Armando and Cristian are as well.

Family is important to Vladimir Guerrero. He is close to his older brother, Wilton, seen here.

The Minors

It is very hard for a baseball player to reach the majors. A young athlete must first **progress** through the minor leagues. There are many different levels of minor-league teams. Each MLB team owns several minor-league ball clubs. The minor leagues provide a chance for baseball players to train for the majors.

However, only a handful of the best minor-league players can **compete** at the major-league level. Most minor-league players never get to play a single major-league inning. Vladimir Guerrero hoped to be one of the lucky ones who make it to the majors when he joined a Dominican Summer League team that was owned by the Montreal Expos in 1993.

Even in the minor leagues, Guerrero became known as a powerful hitter. He has been known to hit the ball so hard that his bat breaks!

Guerrero quickly rose through the minor leagues. In 1996, he joined the Harrisburg Senators. At 20 years old, he was the youngest position player in the Eastern League. Guerrero helped the Senators win the league championship. In fact, he was voted the Most Valuable Player, or MVP, of the entire league. This means that **experts** thought Guerrero had done more to help his team that year than any other player on any other team had.

The Expos had seen enough. They needed a power hitter, so they called Guerrero up from the minors to play in a series against the Atlanta Braves. The Braves were one of the best teams in

Guerrero hit 19 home runs while playing for the Harrisburg Senators in the 1996 season.

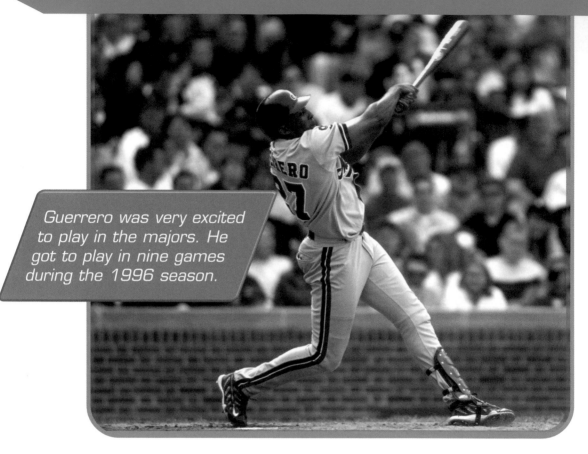

Guerrero was very excited to play in the majors. He got to play in nine games during the 1996 season.

baseball. Guerrero played in his first Major League Baseball game on September 19, 1996. He played well in the series against Atlanta. He even hit a home run against a very good pitcher named Mark Wohlers. Guerrero was ready for the majors!

Guerrero had bad luck in his first full season in Montreal. He was **injured** three times and played in only 90 of the season's 162 games. However, Guerrero played well in those 90 games. His batting average was .302. A batting average is a number that measures how successful a batter is. Guerrero's .302 average means he got a hit about 3 times out of every 10 tries. This is very good. The Expos knew that Guerrero had promise.

Guerrero practiced his baseball skills at spring training with the Expos in 1997, before the opening of his first full year as a professional baseball player.

Along with being a powerful hitter, Guerrero is also a skilled fielder. He plays right field.

Guerrero **fulfilled** that promise in the very next season. He batted .324 and hit 38 home runs and 109 RBIs. RBIs are very important. "RBI" stands for "run batted in." This means that Guerrero was responsible for helping his team score 109 runs.

In 1998, the Guerrero family had a reunion in Montreal. Wilton was traded to the Expos. The brothers moved into an apartment with their mother. She even cooked for them and their teammates!

Guerrero had a great year in 1998. Not only did his brother join him in Montreal, Vladimir also drove in 109 runs, including 38 home runs.

Bad-Ball Hitter

Guerrero became the star of the Expos and one of the best hitters in baseball. He created his own **style** of hitting. He never wore a batting glove. Batting gloves help players grip the bat. Almost everyone uses them. Guerrero's hands were used to hard work, though. He gripped the bat better without a glove.

Guerrero became known as a "bad-ball hitter." Baseball pitchers will often throw outside the **strike zone**. They often do this on purpose to get the batter to swing at a bad pitch. Guerrero is good at hitting ugly pitches. He loves to surprise fielders by hitting balls other players would not swing at, much less hit.

Guerrero is well-known for his skill at hitting bad pitches. Many experts consider him today's best bad-ball hitter.

In his final season with the Expos, Guerrero hit 25 home runs and had a batting average of .330.

The Expos were not a very good team, and in 2003 they decided they could no longer afford to keep Guerrero. The Anaheim Angels were interested in Guerrero. The Angels were a very good team. They had won the World Series in 2002. The World Series is baseball's championship. The Angels hoped Guerrero could help them win another World Series. The owner of the Angels was Arte Moreno. Moreno was the first Latin American to be in charge of a major American sports team. Guerrero **admired** Moreno. He joined the Angels for the 2004 season.

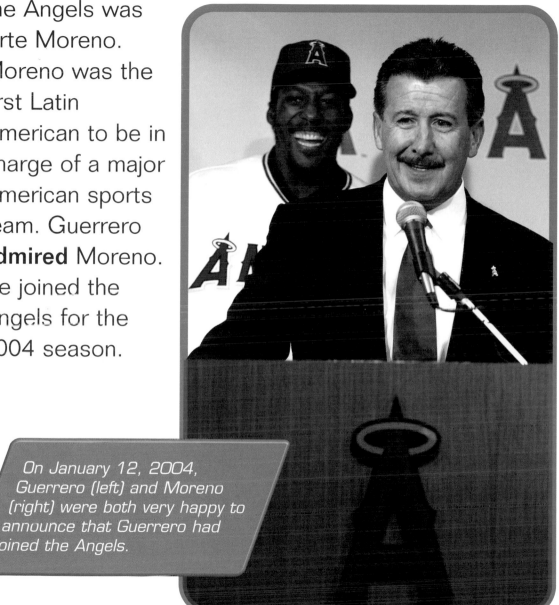

On January 12, 2004, Guerrero (left) and Moreno (right) were both very happy to announce that Guerrero had joined the Angels.

Guerrero was used to being the best player on the team. Now he played for the Angels, and the Angels had a lot of stars. Guerrero played just as well as the more famous ballplayers.

The Angels spent most of the 2004 season trailing the Oakland Athletics. By the time there was only one month left in the season, the Athletics were still in first place. In that final month, Guerrero showed how much he could help his new team. Guerrero had one of the best Septembers in baseball history. He batted .310 and hit 10 home runs and 23 RBIs in just one month. He even hit a total of 6 home runs in the season's final six games! Guerrero's batting average during those final games was .467.

Guerrero got along well with his new teammates. Here, he is celebrating with Chone Figgins after having hit a home run in an important game.

Vladimir Guerrero is known for stealing bases. He stole 15 bases in his first season with the Angels.

Guerrero also played well in the field. He made a famous play that September against the Texas Rangers. He caught a fly ball in right field and threw a runner out. Sports **journalists** and experts compared Guerrero to Roberto Clemente, one of the greatest right fielders of all time.

Guerrero played so well that the Angels finished the season in first place. They beat the Athletics by just one game. Baseball journalists voted Guerrero the American League MVP. Once again, he was the single most valuable player in the whole league.

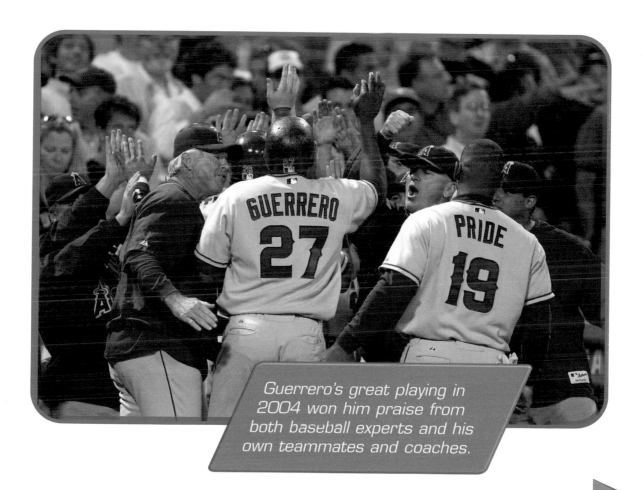

Guerrero's great playing in 2004 won him praise from both baseball experts and his own teammates and coaches.

Guerrero loves the Dominican Republic and tries to spend as much time there as he can.

Guerrero is grateful that he gets to spend his life playing baseball. It is his favorite thing to do. Some major-league players are **criticized** by fans and journalists. They seem to care more about making money than they do about playing baseball. Guerrero is not one of them. He treats baseball like a game instead of a business. This is why Guerrero is so well liked on and off the field.

Guerrero remembers growing up in the Dominican Republic. He remembers that his family and their neighbors were always poor. He often goes home to visit his family. He helped them rebuild their house. He even built a supermarket and a hardware store for his hometown. Guerrero also gave baseball gear to children in his

All-Star Facts

Guerrero enjoys playing baseball games on PlayStation. He loves to bat as himself.

Guerrero is shown here with family members at the 2005 Home Run Derby.

hometown. Children in poor parts of the Dominican Republic play baseball with whatever they can find. Before Guerrero's present, the kids often played with old socks and sticks.

Back in Los Angeles, Guerrero created Vlad's Pad so that poor American children could attend baseball games. Vlad's Pad is a part of the Angels' ballpark reserved just for children. Guerrero gives away more than 100 tickets for every Angels home game. Guerrero also works with the Make-A-Wish Foundation. The Make-A-Wish Foundation is a **charity** that helps sick children and their families.

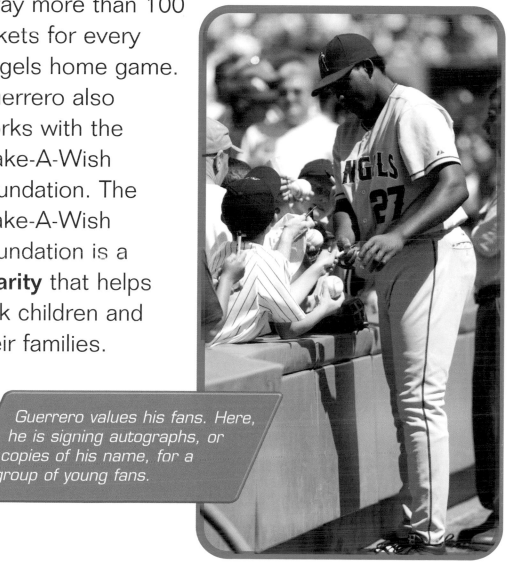

Guerrero values his fans. Here, he is signing autographs, or copies of his name, for a group of young fans.

27

Super Vlad

The shy slugger continues to play well. Guerrero won the 2007 All-Star Game's Home Run Derby. The Home Run Derby is a contest that happens every year at the All-Star Game. The best home run hitters in baseball take turns trying to hit the most home runs. Guerrero did more than hit the most home runs at the 2007 derby. He also hit the longest home run!

The Angels began the 2008 season as one of the best teams in the league. Guerrero's teammates call him Super Vlad because he can hit almost anything. Guerrero does not care what they call him, though. He just loves playing baseball!

Guerrero's skilled fielding, powerful batting, and love of the game make him a great player for fans to watch.

Height: 6' 3" (1.9 m)
Weight: 235 pounds (107 kg)
Team: Los Angeles Angels
                     of Anaheim

Position: Right field
Uniform Number: 27
Bats: Right
Throws: Right
Date of Birth: February 9, 1976

2007 Season Stats

At Bats	Runs	Hits	Home Runs	RBIs	Batting Average
574	89	186	27	125	.324

Career Stats as of October 2007

At Bats	Runs	Hits	Home Runs	RBIs	Batting Average
6,076	1,041	1,972	365	1,177	.313

Glossary

admired (ed-MY-urd) Respected or looked up to.

athlete (ATH-leet) Someone who takes part in sports.

charity (CHER-uh-tee) A group that gives help to the needy.

compete (kum-PEET) To oppose another in a game or test.

criticized (KRIH-tuh-syzd) Found fault with.

experts (EK-sperts) People who know a lot about a subject.

fulfilled (fuhl-FILD) Carried out or finished.

injured (IN-jurd) Harmed or hurt.

journalists (JER-nul-ists) People who gather and write news articles for newspapers or magazines.

professional (pruh-FFSH-nul) Someone who is paid for what he or she does.

progress (pruh-GRES) To move forward.

scouts (SKOWTS) People who help sports teams find new, young players.

strike zone (STRYK ZOHN) The area over home plate through which a ball must pass for it to count as a strike when a batter does not swing.

style (STYL) The way in which something is done.

tradition (truh-DIH-shun) A way of doing something that has been passed down over time.

Index

Web Sites

Due to the changing nature of Internet links, PowerKids Press has developed an online list of Web sites related to the subject of this book. This site is updated regularly. Please use this link to access the list:
www.powerkidslinks.com/asp/vladg/